Liqueurs for Dessert

by

Sandra Wong

MW00720948

Copyright 1988 Sandra J. Wong

All rights reserved. No part of this book may be reproduced without written permission from the author.

ISBN No. 0-88925-884-8

First printing 1988

Printed and bound in Canada
by Friesen Printers — Cloverdale, B.C.

Typeset by The Typeworks — Vancouver, B.C.

Cover photo courtesy of Distillers Co (Canada) Ltd

Liqueurs for Dessert had been a hobby of mine for many years. Had it not been for the encouragement from my family and friends, this would probably not have been written. I would like to thank everyone for their help, from ideas, to testing, to tasting, to editing. I could not have done this alone. I've had a lot of fun writing this book and even more fun making and testing these recipes over the years. I hope you enjoy this as much as I have.

Cheers!

Table of Contents

Grand Marnier

ingredients:

¾	cup	sugar
1		medium size orange
1	26oz	bottle Brandy
1		wooden skewer

method:

Dissolve sugar in Brandy. Pour into a wide mouth jar. Stab the orange with a fork in a number of places. Suspend the orange on a wooden skewer 1 inch above the liquid. Cover tightly with plastic wrap. Let stand for 1 month. Enjoy!

Yield: 1-26oz bottle

Grand Marnier Tarts

ingredients:

2	doz	mini tart shells, baked
⅓	cup	sugar
2	Tbsp	corn starch
		pinch of salt
½	cup	milk
1		egg yolk, beaten
1	Tbsp	butter
1	Tbsp	Grand Marnier
1	10oz	can mandarin orange segments
1	tsp	sugar
½	Tbsp	(½ pkg) unflavoured gelatin
1	Tbsp	Grand Marnier

Grand Marnier Tarts

method:

Drain mandarin oranges, reserving ⅓ cup liquid.

Combine together ⅓ cup sugar, corn starch and salt. Set aside. In the top of a double boiler, heat milk until warm. Stir in sugar mixture. Continue stirring mixture until slightly thickened. Spoon about 3 Tbsp of the hot mixture into the beaten egg yolk, blend well. Return egg yolk mixture to saucepan. Continue stirring until thick and mixture just begins to boil. Remove from heat and stir in butter. Cool for 10 minutes then stir in 1 Tbsp Grand Marnier. When completely cool, spoon into tart shells.

In a small saucepan, combine ⅓ cup liquid from mandarin oranges and 1 tsp sugar. Heat mixture until warm. Sprinkle gelatin on top and stir until dissolved. Remove from heat and stir in 1 Tbsp Grand Marnier. Cool until slightly thickened.

Place a mandarin orange segment on each tart, then spoon gelatin mixture over each orange segment. Place in refrigerator to set gelatin. Refrigerate till ready to serve.

Yield: 2 dozen tarts

Grand Marnier Cheesecake

ingredients:

CRUST

1½	cups	graham wafer crumbs
⅓	cup	sugar
¼	cup	butter or margarine

FILLING

2	8oz	(250g)pkg cream cheese
¾	cup	sugar
4		eggs, separated
4	tsp	Grand Marnier
4	tsp	flour

TOPPING & GLAZE

1	cup	sour cream
2	10oz	cans mandarin orange segments
1	Tbsp	Grand Marnier
⅓	cup	Grand Marnier
1	env	unflavoured gelatin
1	cup	blueberries, optional

method:

Preheat oven to 350° F.

For crust, combine graham wafer crumbs, sugar and melted butter or margarine. Press into a 10 inch springform pan. Bake for 10 minutes. Remove from oven and let cool.

4

Grand Marnier Cheesecake

method (cont'd):

For filling, in a small bowl, beat egg whites until stiff peaks form. Do not over beat. In a large bowl, beat together the cream cheese and sugar, creaming well. Add egg yolks, 4 tsp Grand Marnier and flour. Beat just until blended. Gently fold the egg whites into the cheese mixture. Spread on to crust and bake for 50–55 minutes. Remove from oven and let cool.

For topping, chop ¼ cup mandarin orange segments. Combine the chopped oranges with sour cream and the 1 Tbsp Grand Marnier. Spread on cheesecake. Bake for 10 minutes. Remove from oven and let cool.

For glaze, in a medium bowl, combine remaining mandarin orange segments, juice from both tins and ⅓ cup Grand Marnier. Let stand for 2 hours. Drain fruit, reserving liquid. Heat reserved liquid in a small saucepan. Add gelatin and stir until completely dissolved. Let cool. If desired, arrange the mandarin orange segments and blueberries on top of the cheesecake and pour the cooled gelatin mixture over the top. Refrigerate until set, about 2 hours.

Yield: 10–12 servings

Chocolate Cheese Brownies

ingredients:

2	1oz	sq unsweetened chocolate, melted
⅔	cup	flour
1	tsp	baking powder
¼	tsp	salt
¼	cup	cocoa
¼	cup	butter
1	cup	sugar
2		eggs
¼	cup	milk
1	tsp	vanilla
1	4oz	(125g)pkg cream cheese
¼	cup	sugar
1		egg
¼	cup	Grand Marnier

Chocolate Cheese Brownies

method:

Pre-heat oven to 350° F.

Grease and flour a 8 inch square pan.

Mix together flour, baking powder, salt and cocoa. Set aside. Beat butter and 1 cup sugar until light and fluffy. Beat in 2 eggs, one at a time. Stir in melted chocolate. Add flour mixture alternating with milk, mixing well. Stir in vanilla.

In a small bowl, beat cream cheese until smooth. Add ¼ cup sugar, 1 egg and Grand Marnier, beating well.

Spread about ⅓ of chocolate mixture into prepared pan. Carefully spread cream cheese mixture on top, then remaining chocolate mixture on top of the cream cheese layer. Bake for 30 minutes or until a toothpick inserted in the center comes out barely moist. Remove from oven and cool on a wire rack. Cut into squares and serve.

Yield: 16-2 inch squares.

Chocolate Checkerboard Cake

ingredients:

CHEESECAKE

2	8oz	(250g)pkgs cream cheese
½	cup	sugar
3		eggs
½	cup	whipping cream
⅓	cup	cocoa

CHOCOLATE CAKE

½	cup	cocoa
1	cup	boiling water
½	cup	margarine
1	cup	sugar
3		eggs
¼	cup	Grand Marnier
1½	cups	sifted flour
1	tsp	baking soda
½	tsp	salt
½	tsp	double acting baking powder

Chocolate Checkerboard Cake

method:

Preheat oven to 350° F.

Lightly grease and flour three checkerboard pans. *

In a medium size bowl, beat cream cheese until smooth. Gradually add sugar. Add eggs one at a time, beating well after each. Slowly beat in whipping cream. Add cocoa, mixing well. Put cream cheese mixture aside.

In a small bowl, add water to ½ cup cocoa. Mix well. Let cool.

In a large bowl, cream margarine and sugar. Add eggs, beating well after each. Stir in Grand Marnier. Combine flour, soda, salt and baking powder. Slowly add dry mixture alternately with cocoa mixture, mixing well. Do not over beat.

Pour into checkerboard pans with chocolate cake mixture forming the large circles on two pans. Bake for 35–40 minutes or until a toothpick inserted into the center comes out clean. Let cool for 15 minutes. Remove from pans and cool on wire racks. Place layers on top of each other, alternating. Frost top and sides with whipping cream or chocolate frosting flavoured with Grand Marnier.

Yield: 10–12 servings

*Note: This recipe requires a checkerboard cake pan set.

Chocolate G.M. Cheesecake

ingredients:

CRUST

1½	cups	graham wafer crumbs
2	Tbsp	sugar
¼	cup	cocoa
⅓	cup	butter or margarine, melted

CHEESECAKE

2	8oz	(250g)pkgs cream cheese
½	cup	sugar
3		eggs
1	cup	whipping cream
⅓	cup	cocoa
2	Tbsp	flour
¼	cup	Grand Marnier
		chocolate shavings

Chocolate G.M. Cheesecake

method:

Pre-heat oven to 350° F.

Combine graham wafer crumbs, 2 Tbsp sugar and cocoa. Add the melted butter or margarine, mixing well. Press mixture into a 10 inch springform pan. Bake for 10 minutes. Let cool.

Beat together cream cheese and ½ cup sugar until smooth. Add eggs one at a time, beating well after each. Slowly beat in whipping cream, then cocoa, flour and Grand Marnier. Beat just until mixed. Pour over crust. Bake for 1 hour. Remove from oven and let cool. Sprinkle chocolate shavings on top before serving.

Yield: 10–12 servings

Chocolate G.M. Shortbread

ingredients:

2	cups	butter
⅔	cup	sifted icing sugar
½	cup	cocoa
4	cups	flour, sifted
½	tsp	baking powder
2	Tbsp	Grand Marnier

method:

Pre-heat oven to 300° F.

Cream butter, add icing sugar, creaming well. Gradually add cocoa, flour and baking powder. Stir in Grand Marnier, mixing well, knead together if necessary. Roll out on a floured board and cut into desired shapes. If preferred, a cookie press may be used. Place on ungreased cookie sheets and bake for 8–10 minutes.

Yield: 6 dozen

Irish Cream Liqueur

ingredients:

1	1 oz	sq semi-sweet chocolate
1	can	(300ml) sweetened condensed milk
1	cup	whipping cream
1	cup	whiskey

method:

Melt chocolate, allow to cool.

Mix milk, whipping cream and whiskey together in a blender. Add chocolate and mix well. Pour into a dark bottle and store in the refrigerator. Shake well before using. This liqueur only keeps up to 1 week, so enjoy!!

Yield: approximately 3 cups

Irish Cream Cheesecake

ingredients:

CRUST

1½	cups	graham wafer crumbs
2	Tbsp	sugar
¼	cup	cocoa
⅓	cup	butter or margarine, melted

CHEESECAKE

2	8oz	(250g)pkg cream cheese
½	cup	Irish Cream Liqueur
1	env	unflavoured gelatin
3	Tbsp	hot water
1		egg
2	cups	whipping cream, divided
2	Tbsp	icing sugar
2	Tbsp	Irish Cream Liqueur
		chocolate shavings

Irish Cream Cheesecake

method:

Preheat oven to 350° F.

Combine graham wafer crumbs, 2 Tbsp sugar and cocoa. Add the melted butter or margarine, mixing well. Press mixture into a 10 inch springform pan. Bake for 10 minutes. Let cool.

Beat together cream cheese and ½ cup sugar until smooth. Add egg, beating well.

Sprinkle gelatin over hot water, stirring until dissolved. Stir in ½ cup Irish Cream Liqueur.

Beat 1½ cups whipping cream until stiff peaks form. Do not over beat. Fold in gelatin mixture. Carefully fold whip cream mixture into the cream cheese mixture. Pour over crust. Refrigerate for 2 hours.

Beat ½ cup whipping cream until stiff peaks form. Add icing sugar and 2 Tbsp Irish Cream Liqueur, beating until mixed. Place in piping bag and use to decorate top of cheesecake. Sprinkle chocolate shavings on top. Refrigerate until ready to serve.

Yield: 10–12 servings

Irish Cream Squares
(cover photo)

ingredients:

¾	cup	butter
1⅔	cups	sugar
3		eggs
1	cup	sour cream
1	tsp	vanilla
2	cups	flour
¾	cup	cocoa
2	tsp	double acting baking powder
½	tsp	salt
½	cup	milk
1	pkg	unflavoured gelatin
3	Tbsp	boiling water
2	8 oz	(250g)pkg cream cheese
½	cup	icing sugar
1		egg
3	1 oz	sq semi-sweet chocolate, melted
1	cup	whipping cream
¼	cup	Irish Cream Liqueur

GLAZE

¾	cup	water
¼	cup	Irish Cream Liqueur
½	Tbsp	(½pkg) unflavoured gelatin
8–10		whole strawberries

method:

Preheat oven to 350 deg. F.

Grease and flour three 8 inch square cake pans.

Irish Cream Squares

method (cont'd)

For chocolate cake, cream butter. Add sugar, creaming well. Add the 3 eggs one at a time, beating well. Mix in sour cream and vanilla. Sift together flour, cocoa, baking powder and salt. Add sifted mixture to creamed mixture alternating with milk. Mix well. Divide batter into the three prepared pans and bake for 35–40 minutes or until a toothpick inserted into the center comes out clean. Remove from oven and let cool. Cut each layer in half. Set aside while preparing filling.

For chocolate mousse filling, dissolve 1 pkg gelatin in 3 Tbsp boiling water. Set aside.

Beat cream cheese until smooth. Gradually add icing sugar. Add egg and beat well. Beat in melted chocolate, whipping cream and 1/4 cup Irish Cream Liqueur. Add dissolved gelatin and beat well. Place chocolate mousse in the refrigerator for 1/2 hour to set. Spread chocolate mousse filling between each layer and on the top. Refrigerate until ready to serve.

In a small saucepan, combine 3/4 cup water and 1/4 cup Irish Cream Liqueur. Heat mixture until warm. Sprinkle gelatin on top and stir until dissolved. Remove from heat and cool for 10 minutes.

Cut the cake into squares. Place a strawberry on each square and pour gelatin mixture over top.

Yield: 8–10 servings

Kahlua

ingredients:

2	cups	water
3	Tbsp	instant coffee
4	cups	sugar
¼		vanilla bean
1	26 oz	bottle Brandy

method:

Boil together water and coffee. Add sugar and stir until dissolved. Let mixture cool for 30 minutes then add Brandy and mix well. Pour into a bottle and add the vanilla bean. Let stand for 1 month in a cool place. Then enjoy!

Yield: approx. 42oz

Kahlua Butter Tarts

ingredients:

2	doz	tart shells, unbaked
½	cup	butter
1	cup	brown sugar
2		eggs
½	cup	light corn syrup
1	cup	raisins
¼	cup	Kahlua

method:

Preheat oven to 375° F.

Cream together butter and sugar, creaming well. Beat in eggs one at a time. Add corn syrup, raisins and Kahlua, mixing well. Spoon into tart shells and bake for 25–30 minutes or until a knife inserted in the centre comes out clean.

Yield: 24 tarts

Kahlua Mousse Torte

ingredients:

1¼	cups	graham wafer crumbs
2	Tbsp	sugar
¼	cup	cocoa
¼	cup	butter or margarine, melted
2	8oz	(250g)pkgs cream cheese
½	cup	sugar
3		eggs
3	1oz	sq semi-sweet chocolate, melted
¼	cup	Kahlua
1	1oz	sq semi-sweet chocolate, chopped
2	cups	whipping cream
2	Tbsp	Kahlua
2		eggs, separated
2	1oz	sq semi-sweet chocolate, melted
2	Tbsp	sugar
		chocolate shavings

method:

Preheat oven to 350° F.

Combine graham wafer crumbs, 2 Tbsp sugar, cocoa
and the melted butter or margarine. Mix well. Press
mixture into a 9 inch springform pan. Bake for 10
minutes. Let cool.

Kahlua Mousse Torte

method (cont'd):

Beat together cream cheese and ½ cup sugar until smooth. Add the 3 whole eggs, beating well after each. Slowly beat in 3 squares melted chocolate and ¼ cup Kahlua. Pour over crust and bake at 325° F. for 35–40 minutes. Remove from oven and let cool for 30 minutes.

Sprinkle the 1 square chopped chocolate over the baked cheese layer. Chocolate will melt slightly. Let stand while preparing the next layer.

Whip whipping cream until thick. Add 2 Tbsp Kahlua and beat until stiff peaks form. Do not over beat!

Beat 2 egg yolks until thick. Add 2 squares melted chocolate, beating well. Set aside. In a separate bowl, beat 2 egg whites until thick. Add 2 Tbsp sugar beating until stiff peaks form. Fold in egg yolk mixture and ½ of the whipped cream mixture. Spread on top of the chocolate cheesecake layer. Carefully spread remaining whipping cream on top. Sprinkle chocolate shavings on whipped cream. Refrigerate until ready to serve.

Yield: 8–10 servings

Chocolate Kahlua Cheesecake

ingredients:

CRUST
1½	cups	chocolate wafer crumbs
⅓	cup	butter or margarine, melted

CHEESECAKE
2	8oz	(250g)pkgs cream cheese
⅔	cup	sugar
2	Tbsp	flour
3		eggs
1	cup	whipping cream
4	1oz	sq semi-sweet chocolate, melted
¼	cup	Kahlua

TOPPING
1	cup	sour cream
2	Tbsp	Kahlua
2	Tbsp	sugar
		chocolate shavings

Chocolate Kahlua Cheesecake

method:

Preheat oven to 350° F.

Mix together chocolate wafer crumbs and the melted butter or margarine. Press mixture into a 8 inch springform pan. Bake for 10 minutes. Remove from oven and let cool.

Beat together cream cheese and ⅔ cup sugar until smooth. Add flour, beating well. Add eggs one at a time, beating well after each. Slowly beat in whipping cream, melted chocolate and ¼ cup Kahlua. Beat just until mixed. Pour over crust. Bake for 65–70 minutes. Remove from oven.

Mix together sour cream, 2 Tbsp sugar and 2 Tbsp Kahlua. Spread on cheesecake. Return to oven and bake at 225° F. for 10 minutes. Remove from oven and let cool.

Sprinkle chocolate shavings on top before serving.

Yield: 8–10 servings

Kahlua Marshmallow Fudge

ingredients:

3	cups	semi-sweet chocolate chips
1	can	(300ml) sweetened condensed milk
1	Tbsp	margarine
¼	cup	Kahlua
1	cup	miniature marshmallows

method:

Line an 8 inch square pan with wax paper.

In a heavy saucepan, mix together, chocolate chips, milk, and margarine. Over low heat, stir constantly, until chocolate chips are melted. Remove from heat and mix in Kahlua and marshmallows. Spread mixture onto prepared pan. Chill for 3 hours or until firm. Remove from pan. Peel off wax paper and cut into squares.

Yield: 16-2 inch squares

Chocolate Cheese Squares

ingredients:

2	cups	chocolate wafer crumbs
¾	cup	butter, melted
3	8oz	(250g)pkg cream cheese
⅔	cup	sugar
2		eggs
4	Tbsp	flour
2	cups	whipping cream
4	1oz	sq semi-sweet chocolate, melted
2	Tbsp	Kahlua
		chocolate curls

method:

Preheat oven to 350° F.

Mix together chocolate wafer crumbs and melted butter. Press into the bottom of a 9 × 12 inch cake pan. Bake for 15 minutes. Remove from oven and let cool.

Beat cream cheese until smooth. Gradually add sugar. Add eggs one at a time beating well. On low speed, beat in flour, whipping cream, melted chocolate and Kahlua, mixing well. Pour over crust and bake for 30–35 minutes. Remove from oven and let cool.

Refrigerate for 2 hours before serving. Top with chocolate curls and cut into squares.

Yield: 24-1½ × 2 inch squares

Kahlua Cheese Squares

ingredients:

1¼	cups	chocolate wafer crumbs
¼	cup	butter, melted
1	8oz	(250g)pkg cream cheese
⅓	cup	sugar
1		egg
2	Tbsp	flour
1	cup	whipping cream
2	Tbsp	Kahlua
		chocolate curls

method:

Preheat oven to 350° F.

Mix together chocolate wafer crumbs and butter. Press into bottom of a 9 inch square pan. Bake for 10 minutes. Remove from oven and let cool.

Beat cream cheese until smooth. Gradually add sugar. Add egg and beat well. On low speed, beat in flour, whipping cream and Kahlua, mixing well. Pour over crust and bake for 25 minutes. Let cool. Refrigerate for 2 hours before serving. Top with chocolate curls and cut into squares.

Yield: 16-2¼ inch squares

Blueberry Amaretto Mousse

ingredients:

1	cup	blueberries, fresh or frozen
¼	cup	Amaretto Liqueur
1	cup	whipping cream
½	cup	icing sugar
1		egg white
1	tsp	cream of tartar

method:

Chill 4 champagne flute glasses.

If using frozen blueberries, let thaw before pureeing.

Puree blueberries, mix in Amaretto Liqueur. Set aside.

Whip whipping cream until thick. Gradually add icing sugar, whipping until stiff peaks form. Do not over beat! Set aside ½ cup for garnish.

In another bowl, beat egg white and cream of tartar until stiff peaks form. Fold into whipped cream mixture. Also, fold in blueberry mixture. Do not stir. Spoon into chilled glasses, garnish with whipped cream and refrigerate till ready to serve.

Yield: 4 servings

Blueberry Amaretto Squares

ingredients:

1	cup	graham wafer crumbs
½	cup	rolled oats
⅓	cup	butter or margarine, melted
1	8oz	(250g)pkg cream cheese
⅓	cup	sugar
1		egg
2	Tbsp	Amaretto Liqueur
1	Tbsp	flour
1	cup	sour cream
1½	cups	blueberries, fresh or frozen

method:

Preheat oven to 350° F.

Lightly grease a 9 inch square cake pan.

Combine together, graham wafer crumbs, rolled oats and melted butter or margarine. Press mixture into prepared pan. Bake for 10 minutes.

Beat together cream cheese and sugar until smooth. Add egg and beat well. Beat in Amaretto and flour on low speed. Gently fold in sour cream. Fold in blueberries. Pour on to crust and bake for 25–30 minutes. Remove from oven and cool completely before serving.

Yield: 9-3 inch squares

Amaretto Shortbread Balls

ingredients:

2	cups	butter
¾	cup	icing sugar, sifted
2	Tbsp	Amaretto Liqueur
4	cups	flour, sifted
½	tsp	baking powder
		chopped almonds

method:

Preheat oven to 325° F.

Cream butter, gradually add icing sugar, creaming well. Add Amaretto Liqueur. Gradually, add flour and baking powder. Mix well. Turn out on to floured pastry board and knead dough together. Form dough into small balls and roll in chopped almonds. Place on cookie sheet and bake for 12 to 15 minutes or until slightly brown around edges. Remove from cookie sheet and place on wire rack to cool.

Yield: 5 dozen

Fresh Strawberry Cake

ingredients:

5		eggs, separated
½	tsp	cream of tartar
¾	cup	water
1	cup	sugar
1¾	cups	flour, sifted
1¼	tsp	double acting baking powder
¼	tsp	salt
1	tsp	Amaretto Liqueur
3	cups	fresh strawberries
2	cups	whipping cream
¼	cup	Amaretto Liqueur
¼	cup	icing sugar

method:

In a large bowl, beat egg whites and cream of tartar until stiff peaks form. Do not over beat! Set aside.

In another large bowl beat egg yolks and water until thick and foamy. Gradually add 1 cup sugar, beating well.

Fresh Strawberry Cake

method (cont'd):

Sift together flour, baking powder and salt. Gradually add to egg yolk mixture on low speed. Stir in 1 tsp Amaretto Liqueur and mix well.

Fold egg white mixture into egg yolk mixture carefully, just until combined. Pour into a 9 inch ungreased tube cake pan. Bake for 40 minutes or until a toothpick inserted into the center comes out clean. Remove from oven and hang upside down until cool. Carefully split cake horizontally into 3 layers.

Wash and hull strawberries. Set aside 1 cup whole berries for garnish. Slice remaining berries.

Beat whipping cream until slightly thickened. Gradually add ¼ cup Amaretto Liqueur and icing sugar. Beat until peaks stand up. Be careful not to over beat. Set aside ⅓ of whipped cream for top and sides. Spread remaining whipped cream and sliced strawberries between the 3 layers of cake. Ice top and sides. Pipe a rim around edge of cake and garnish top with the whole strawberries. Refrigerate until ready to serve.

Yield: 8–10 servings

Strawberry Amaretto Cheesecake

ingredients:

CRUST

1½	cups	graham wafer crumbs
2	Tbsp	sugar
¼	cup	cocoa
⅓	cup	butter or margarine, melted

CHEESECAKE

2	8oz	(250g)pkgs cream cheese
¾	cup	sugar
3		eggs
1	cup	strawberries, fresh or frozen
2	env	unflavoured gelatin
½	cup	hot water
¾	cup	Amaretto Liqueur
2	cups	whipping cream, divided
2	Tbsp	icing sugar
2	Tbsp	Amaretto Liqueur
		chocolate shavings

Strawberry Amaretto Cheesecake

method:

Preheat oven to 350° F.

Combine graham wafer crumbs, 2 Tbsp sugar and cocoa. Add the melted butter or margarine, mix well. Press mixture into a 10 inch springform pan. Bake for 10 minutes. Let cool.

Beat together cream cheese and ¾ cup sugar until smooth. Add eggs one at a time, beating well after each. Slowly beat in strawberries. If using frozen berries, be sure berries are thawed.

Sprinkle gelatin over hot water, stirring until dissolved. Stir in ¾ cup Amaretto Liqueur.

Beat 1½ cups whipping cream until stiff peaks form. Do not over beat. Fold in gelatin mixture. Carefully fold whip cream mixture into the cream cheese mixture. Pour over crust. Refrigerate for 2 hours.

Beat ½ cup whipping cream until stiff peaks form. Add icing sugar and 2 Tbsp Amaretto Liqueur, beating until mixed. Place in piping bag and use to decorate top of cheesecake. Sprinkle chocolate shavings on top. Refrigerate till ready to serve.

Yield: 10–12 servings

Fresh Strawberry Pie

ingredients:

1		9 inch baked pie shell
10	cups	fresh strawberries, divided
⅓	cup	sugar
1	cup	cold water
⅓	cup	cornstarch
¼	cup	Brandy
		sweetened whipped cream

method:

Wash and hull strawberries.

Set aside 6 cups strawberries. Mash remaining berries. Strain, reserving juice in a saucepan. Add water to give 2 cups. Stir in sugar.

Mix together 1 cup cold water and corn starch. Stir into juice and heat over medium heat until thickened and mixture begins to boil. Remove from heat, stir in Brandy and let cool.

Stack remaining 6 cups strawberries in pie shell. Spoon strawberry mixture over berries and chill in refrigerator for 1 hour or longer. Top with whipping cream before serving.

Yield: 6 servings

Cherry Surprises

ingredients:

1	cup	butter
½	cup	icing sugar, sifted
2	cups	flour, sifted
½	tsp	baking powder
¼	tsp	salt
½	cup	Brandy
25–30		red cherry halves

method:

Preheat oven to 325° F.

Soak cherries in Brandy and let stand for at least 1 hour before using. Drain.

Cream butter, gradually add icing sugar, creaming well. Gradually, add flour, baking powder and salt. Mix well.

Turn out on to floured pastry board and knead dough together. Form dough into a small ball, flatten, place a cherry in the centre and roll into a ball again. Place on cookie sheet and bake for 15 minutes or until lightly brown on the bottom. Remove from cookie sheet and let cool on wire rack.

Yield: 25–30 medium size cookies

Fruitcake

ingredients:

3	cups	flour
3	tsp	baking powder
2	tsp	ground cinnamon
1	tsp	salt
½	tsp	ground nutmeg
5	cups	diced deluxe mixed fruit
3	cups	raisins
1½	cups	pecan halves
4		eggs
1¾	cups	packed brown sugar
1	cup	orange juice
¾	cup	butter or margarine melted and cooled
¼	cup	molasses
½	cup	mixture of orange juice and Brandy

Fruitcake

method:

Preheat oven to 300° F.

Line bottom and sides of 3 8×2×4 inch loaf pans with wax paper.

In a large bowl, sift together flour, baking powder, cinnamon, salt and nutmeg. Add fruits, raisins and nuts, mixing well. Set aside.

Beat eggs at high speed until foamy and pale in colour. Gradually add brown sugar, beating well. Reduce speed and beat in orange juice, butter or margarine and molasses. Beat until well blended. Pour over fruit mixture and stir until mixed. Using a large spoon, spoon batter into prepared pans. Bake for 1½ hours or until a toothpick inserted in the center comes out clean.

Cool cakes on a wire rack. Remove from pans. Wrap cakes in cheesecloth and baste with orange juice and Brandy mixture. Wrap in foil and store in a cool dry place 3–4 weeks to mellow. Cakes may be basted weekly if desired.

Yield: 3 small loaf cakes

Black Forest Cake

ingredients:

¾	cup	butter
1⅔	cups	sugar
3		eggs
1	cup	sour cream
1	tsp	vanilla
2	cups	flour
¾	cup	cocoa
2	tsp	double acting baking powder
½	tsp	salt
½	cup	milk
½	cup	Brandy
1	19oz	(540ml)can cherry pie filling
3	cups	whipping cream
¼	cup	icing sugar
2	Tbsp	Brandy
		maraschino cherries
		chocolate curls

Black Forest Cake

method:

Preheat oven to 350° F.

Grease and flour three 8 inch round cake pans.

Cream butter. Add sugar, creaming well. Add eggs one at a time, beating well. Mix in sour cream and vanilla.

Sift together flour, cocoa, baking powder and salt. Add sifted mixture to creamed mixture alternating with milk. Mix well. Divide batter into the three prepared pans and bake for 35–40 minutes or until a toothpick inserted into the center comes out clean. Remove from oven and let cool.

Beat whipping cream until thick. Add 2 Tbsp Brandy and icing sugar. Whip until soft peaks form. Do not over beat!!

When cake is completely cool, place one layer on a plate. Baste cake with Brandy, spread cherry pie filling on this layer. Place second cake layer on top of cherries. Baste this cake with Brandy, then spread about 1 cup of the whipped cream on this layer. Place third cake layer on top of whipping cream. Baste with remaining Brandy. Ice top and sides with remaining whipped cream. Garnish with maraschino cherries and chocolate curls. Refrigerate till serving.

Yield: 8–10 servings

Black Forest Ice Cream Pie

ingredients:

1½	cups	chocolate wafer crumbs
⅓	cup	butter or margarine, melted
4	cups	chocolate ice cream, divided
2	cups	vanilla ice cream
1	19oz	(540ml)can cherry pie filling
¼	cup	Brandy
		whipping cream
		maraschino cherries
		chocolate curls

Black Forest Ice Cream Pie

method:

This dessert should be made a day ahead.

Preheat oven to 350° F.

Mix together chocolate wafer crumbs and the melted butter or margarine. Press mixture into a 9 inch springform pan. Bake for 10 minutes. Let cool. Place in freezer for 15 minutes.

Soften ½ of the chocolate ice cream. Spread on the chocolate crust. Return to freezer and freeze for 1 hour or until firm.

Mix together cherry pie filling and Brandy. Spread on top of chocolate ice cream. Return to freezer for 1 hour.

Soften the vanilla ice cream. Spread on top of the cherry layer. Return to freezer for 1 hour or until firm.

Soften remaining ½ of the chocolate ice cream. Spread on top of vanilla ice cream. Return to freezer and freeze until serving time. Just before serving, garnish with whipping cream, maraschino cherries and chocolate curls.

Hint: for ease in softening ice cream, place in microwave for 1 minute on defrost setting.

Yield: 10–12 servings

Brandy Orange Cheesecake

ingredients:

BASE

1½	cups	vanilla wafer crumbs
½	cup	butter, melted
2	Tbsp	orange rind

FILLING

2	8oz	(250g)pkgs cream cheese
½	cup	sugar
3		eggs
1	cup	whipping cream
2	Tbsp	orange juice
2	tsp	orange rind
3	Tbsp	Brandy
		orange rind
		whipping cream

method:

Preheat oven to 350° F.

Mix together wafer crumbs and orange rind. Add butter mixing well. Press into a 9 inch springform pan. Bake for 10 minutes. Let cool.

Beat cream cheese until smooth. Gradually add sugar. Add eggs one at a time. Slowly beat in whipping cream. Add orange juice, rind and brandy. Mix well. Pour on top of crust. Sprinkle with remaining orange rind. Bake for 1 hour. Remove from oven and let cool. Garnish with orange rind and whipping cream. Refrigerate till serving.

Yield: 8–10 servings

Brandy Cherry Pound Cake

ingredients:

2	cups	glazed cherries
1	cup	Brandy
2¼	cups	flour
½	tsp	salt
1½	tsp	baking powder
1	cup	butter, at room temperature
1¼	cups	sugar
4		eggs

method:

Combine cherries and Brandy and let stand overnight.

Preheat oven to 350° F.

Grease and flour a 9 inch loaf pan.

Drain cherries and set aside.

Sift together flour, salt and baking powder. Set aside.

Beat butter, gradually add sugar and beat until light and fluffy. Add eggs, one at a time beating well after each. On low speed, add flour mixture mixing well. Fold in cherries. Pour into prepared pan and bake for 60 minutes or until a toothpick inserted in the center comes out clean. Remove from oven and let cool.

Yield: 1–9 inch loaf

Pineapple Cheesecake

ingredients:

BASE

1½	cups	graham wafer crumbs
½	cup	butter, melted

FILLING

2	8oz	(250g)pkgs cream cheese
½	cup	sugar
3		eggs
1	cup	whipping cream
1	14oz	(398ml)can crushed pineapple

GLAZE

1	14oz	(398ml)can sliced pineapple
1	env	unflavoured gelatin
¼	cup	Rum

Pineapple Cheesecake

method:

Pre-heat oven to 350° F.

Mix together wafer crumbs and butter. Press into a 9 inch springform pan. Bake for 10 minutes. Let cool.

Drain crushed pineapple, reserving juice. Beat cream cheese until smooth. Gradually, add sugar. Add eggs one at a time. Beat well. Slowly beat in whipping cream. Stir in crushed pineapple. Pour over crust and bake for 50 to 60 minutes. Remove from oven and let cool.

Drain sliced pineapple, reserving juice. To reserved pineapple juice, add just enough water to give 2 cups. Heat liquid in saucepan until it begins to boil. Remove from burner and add gelatin, stirring until gelatin is completely dissolved. Let cool. Add Rum to mixture and stir well. Let stand to thicken.

Arrange pineapple rings on top of cheesecake. When gelatin mixture is thickened, pour over pineapple rings. Refrigerate until ready to serve.

Yield: 8 servings

Pina Colada Gelatin

ingredients:

1	14 oz	can sliced pineapple rings
2	pkgs	(85g)ea Jell-O Pineapple Jelly Powder
1	env	unflavoured gelatin
2	cups	boiling water
1	cup	cold water
2	cups	vanilla ice cream
½	cup	Light Rum
1	cup	shredded coconut
		pineapple rings
		shredded coconut

Pina Colada Gelatin

method:

Drain sliced pineapple rings. Set aside.

Dissolve Pineapple Jelly Powder and unflavoured gelatin in boiling water, stirring until powder is dissolved. Stir in cold water. Spoon in vanilla ice cream and stir until ice cream is dissolved. Stir in Rum and coconut.

Place pineapple rings on bottom of a 6 cup gelatin mold. Pour gelatin mixture over pineapple rings. Chill for 4 hours or until set. To serve, dip mold into warm water for 25 seconds and invert on to a serving plate. Garnish with pineapple rings and shredded coconut.

Yield: 6–8 servings

Rum'n Lemon Bars

ingredients:

CRUST

1	cup	flour
½	cup	butter
3	Tbsp	sugar

FILLING

2		eggs
1	cup	sugar
¼	cup	flour
½	tsp	baking powder
½	tsp	grated lemon rind
¼	cup	fresh lemon juice
2	Tbsp	Light Rum

method:

Preheat oven to 350° F.

For crust, combine flour, butter and sugar. Using a pastry blender or 2 forks, mix until crumbly. Press mixture into an unbuttered 8 inch square pan. Bake for 20 minutes. Remove from oven.

For filling, beat eggs with a fork. Stir in sugar. Add remaining ingredients, mixing well. Pour over crust. Bake for 25–30 minutes. Filling should be slightly firm and lightly browned around the edges.

Yield: 16-2 inch squares

Grapefruit Cooler

ingredients:

2	cups	grapefruit juice
1	8oz	can diet 7up
½	cup	Light Rum
1		lime, sliced
		ice cubes
4		tall glasses, chilled

method:

Mix together grapefruit juice, 7up and Rum in a large jug. Place ice cubes and 2–3 slices of lime in each glass. Pour grapefruit mixture into glasses. Stir and serve.

Yield: 4 servings

Fresh Fruit'n Rum Flan

ingredients:

1		12 inch sponge cake flan
1	4oz	(125g) pkg cream cheese
2	Tbsp	sugar
1		egg
2	Tbsp	Light Rum
1		large peach, peeled and sliced
½	cup	blueberries
¼	cup	lemon juice
2	Tbsp	Light Rum
¼	cup	sugar
¾	cup	water
½	env	unflavoured gelatin

method:

Beat together cream cheese and sugar until smooth. Add egg, 2 Tbsp sugar and 2 Tbsp Light Rum, mixing well. Spread on flan.

Arrange fruit on top of cream cheese.

In a small saucepan, combine lemon juice, 2 Tbsp rum, ¼ cup sugar and water. Mix well. Add gelatin and cook over medium heat, stirring constantly until mixture begins to boil. Remove from heat and let cool. When gelatin mixture is slightly thickened, slowly pour over fruits on flan. Refrigerate for 2 hours before serving.

Yield: 8–10 servings

Eggnog Cheesecake

ingredients:

BASE

1½	cups	graham wafer crumbs
½	cup	butter, melted

FILLING

2	8oz	(250g)pkgs cream cheese
½	cup	sugar
4		eggs
½	cup	whipping cream
1	cup	eggnog
¼	cup	Rum
		sweetened whipped cream
		nutmeg

method:

Preheat oven to 350° F.

Mix together wafer crumbs and butter. Press into a 9 inch springform pan. Bake for 10 minutes. Remove from oven and let cool.

Beat cream cheese until smooth. Gradually, add sugar. Add eggs one at a time. Beat well. Slowly beat in whipping cream, eggnog and Rum. Pour over crust and bake for 50 to 60 minutes. Remove from oven and let cool.

Before serving, sprinkle nutmeg over cheesecake and pipe whipped cream around the edge.

Yield: 10 servings

Mud Pie

ingredients:

1½	cups	chocolate wafer crumbs
⅓	cup	butter or margarine, melted
2	cups	chocolate ice cream
2	Tbsp	Kahlua
4	cups	coffee ice cream
2	Tbsp	Irish Cream Liqueur

CHOCOLATE SAUCE

½	cup	whipping cream
3	1oz	sq unsweetened chocolate
¼	cup	sugar
¼	cup	corn syrup
1	Tbsp	butter
2	Tbsp	Irish Cream Liqueur
		sweetened whipped cream
		slivered almonds

Mud Pie

method:

This dessert should be made a day ahead.

Preheat oven to 350° F.

Mix together chocolate wafer crumbs and the melted butter or margarine. Press mixture into a 9 inch springform pan. Bake for 10 minutes. Let cool. Place in freezer for 15 minutes.

Soften the chocolate ice cream. Add Kahlua, mixing well. Spread on the chocolate crust. Return to freezer and freeze for 1 hour or until firm.

Soften the coffee ice cream. Add Irish Cream Liqueur, mixing well. Spread on top of chocolate ice cream layer. Return to freezer.

For chocolate sauce, mix together whipping cream, chocolate, sugar and corn syrup in a saucepan. Heat over medium heat, stirring constantly until chocolate melts and mixture is slightly thickened. Remove from heat and stir in butter and Irish Cream Liqueur.

Just before serving, spoon chocolate sauce over slices and garnish with whipped cream and slivered almonds.

Hint: for ease in softening ice cream, place in microwave for 1 minute on defrost setting.

Yield: 10–12 servings

B52 Ice Cream Pie

ingredients:

1½	cups	chocolate wafer crumbs
⅓	cup	butter or margarine, melted
2	cups	coffee ice cream
2	Tbsp	Kahlua
2	cups	vanilla ice cream
2	Tbsp	Irish Cream Liqueur
2	cups	orange ice cream
2	Tbsp	Grand Marnier
		sweetened whipped cream for garnish

B52 Ice Cream Pie

method:

This dessert should be made a day ahead.

Preheat oven to 350° F.

Mix together chocolate wafer crumbs and the melted butter or margarine. Press mixture into a 9 inch springform pan. Bake for 10 minutes. Let cool. Place in freezer for 15 minutes.

Soften the coffee ice cream. Add Kahlua, mixing well. Spread on the chocolate crust. Return to freezer and freeze for 1 hour or until firm.

Soften the vanilla ice cream. Add Irish Cream, mixing well. Spread on top of coffee ice cream layer. Return to freezer and freeze for 1 hour or until firm.

Soften the orange ice cream. Add Grand Marnier, mixing well. Spread on top of the vanilla ice cream layer. Return to freezer and freeze for 1 hour or until firm.

Just before serving, garnish with whipped cream.

Hint: for ease in softening ice cream, place in microwave for 1 minute on defrost setting.

Yield: 10–12 servings

B52 Bars

ingredients:

CRUST

2	cups	graham wafer crumbs
¼	cup	sugar
½	cup	cocoa
¾	cup	butter, melted

FIRST LAYER

2	8oz	(250g)pkgs cream cheese
½	cup	sugar
2		eggs
3	1oz	sq semi-sweet chocolate, melted
¼	cup	Kahlua

SECOND LAYER

1	cup	whipping cream
1	8oz	(250g)pkg cream cheese
2	Tbsp	sugar
¼	cup	Irish Cream Liqueur

THIRD LAYER

2	10oz	(284ml)cans mandarin orange segments
1	env	unflavoured gelatin
¼	cup	Grand Marnier

method:

Preheat oven to 350° F.

Combine together graham wafer crumbs, ¼ cup sugar, cocoa and butter. Mix well. Press mixture into a 9 × 12 inch cake pan. Bake for 15 minutes. Remove from oven and let cool.

B52 Bars

method (cont'd):

For first layer, beat 2 pkgs cream cheese, add ½ cup sugar and beat until smooth. Beat in eggs one at a time, then melted chocolate and Kahlua, beating until well blended. Pour over crust and bake for 35–40 minutes or until a toothpick inserted in the center comes out clean. Remove from oven and allow to cool.

For second layer, whip whipping cream until stiff peaks form. Do not over beat. Set aside.

In another bowl beat 1 pkg cream cheese until smooth. Add 2 Tbsp sugar and Irish Cream Liqueur, beating until well blended. Fold cream cheese mixture into whipped cream. Spread on first layer. Be sure the first layer is completely cooled or the whipped cream layer will melt. Refrigerate while preparing the next layer.

For third layer, drain mandarin oranges, reserving liquid. To reserved liquid, add water to give 2 cups. Heat liquid in saucepan just until it begins to boil. Remove from burner and add gelatin. Stir until gelatin is completely dissolved. Allow to cool. Add Grand Marnier, stirring well. Arrange mandarin orange segments on top of second layer. When gelatin mixture begins to thicken, pour over mandarin orange segments. Refrigerate till serving.

Yield: 18-3 × 2 inch squares

Peach Cake

ingredients:

4		eggs, separated
½	tsp	cream of tarter
¾	cup	water
1	cup	sugar
1½	cups	flour, sifted
1½	tsp	double acting baking powder
¼	tsp	salt
½	tsp	vanilla extract
1	28oz	can sliced peaches
¼	cup	sugar
¼	cup	Peach Schnapps
2	cups	whipping cream
¼	cup	icing sugar
¼	cup	Peach Schnapps

method:

Preheat oven to 350° F.

In a large bowl, beat egg whites and cream of tarter until stiff peaks form. Set aside.

In another large bowl, beat egg yolks and water until thick and foamy (about 5 minutes on high speed). Gradually add 1 cup sugar, beating well.

Sift together flour, baking powder and salt. Gradually add to egg yolk mixture on low speed. Stir in vanilla and mix well.

Peach Cake

method (cont'd):

Fold egg white mixture into egg yolk mixture carefully, just until combined. Pour into a 9 inch ungreased tube cake pan. Bake for 40 minutes or until a toothpick inserted into the cake comes out clean. Remove from oven and hang upside down until cool. Carefully split cake horizontally into 3 layers.

Drain peaches, puree in blender. Add ¼ cup sugar and cook over medium heat until mixture is slightly thickened and begins to boil. Remove from heat and allow to cool. Stir in ¼ cup Peach Schnapps.

Beat whipping cream until slightly thickened. Gradually add icing sugar, then ¼ cup Peach Schnapps. Beat until peaks stand up.

Set aside ⅓ of peach mixture. To the remainder, fold in 1½ cups whipped cream mixture. Spread this mixture between the 3 layers. Spread remaining whipping cream on the sides of the cake. Pipe a rim around the top outside and inside edges. Spread remaining peach mixture on top, between the two edges. Refrigerate until ready to serve.

Yield: 8–10 servings

Peaches'n Cream

ingredients:

2	pkgs	(85g)ea Jell-O Cherry Jelly Powder
1	env	unflavoured gelatin
2	cups	boiling water
1½	cups	cold water
1	28oz	can sliced peaches
2	pkgs	(85g)ea Jell-O Peach Jelly Powder
1	env	unflavoured gelatin
2	cups	boiling water
1½	cups	cold water
2	cups	vanilla ice cream
¼	cup	Peach Schnapps

Peaches'n Cream

method:

First Layer:
Dissolve Cherry Jelly Powder and 1 env unflavoured gelatin in boiling water. Stir until powder is dissolved. Stir in 1½ cups cold water. Pour mixture into a 12 cup gelatin mold or bundt pan. Chill. Drain peaches. When mixture is slightly thickened add ½ of the sliced peaches into the jelly mixture. Be sure the peaches are covered with the gelatin mixture. Chill for 1 hour or until gelatin is set.

Second layer:
Dissolve Peach Jelly Powder and 1 env unflavoured gelatin in boiling water. Stir until powder is dissolved. Stir in 1¼ cups cold water. Stir in ice cream, stirring until blended. Stir in Peach Schnapps. Pour over first layer in mold. Add remaining peaches. Chill for 4 hours or until set. To serve, dip mold into warm water for 25 seconds and invert onto a large serving plate.

Yield: 12–14 servings

Creme De Menthe Bars

ingredients:

BASE

3	Tbsp	butter
3	Tbsp	cocoa
2	cups	miniature marshmallows
2	cups	rice krispies cereal

FILLING

½	cup	butter
¼	cup	custard powder
1	1oz	sq semi-sweet chocolate, melted
2	Tbsp	milk
1	Tbsp	Creme de Menthe Liqueur
2	cups	icing sugar, sifted

TOPPING

5	1oz	sq semi-sweet chocolate
2	Tbsp	butter
3	Tbsp	Creme de Menthe Liqueur
1	cup	miniature marshmallows

Creme De Menthe Bars

method:

In a heavy saucepan, melt 3 Tbsp butter and cocoa. Add 2 cups marshmallows, stirring until melted. Remove from heat. Stir in rice krispies, mixing well. Press mixture into a 8 inch square pan.

Beat butter until smooth and creamy. Add custard powder, 1 sq melted chocolate, milk and 1 Tbsp Creme de Menthe Liqueur mixing well. Gradually beat in icing sugar, beating until light and fluffy, about 5 minutes. Spread on rice krispie base. Refrigerate while preparing next layer.

Melt 5 sq chocolate and 2 Tbsp butter. Stir in 3 Tbsp Creme de Menthe Liqueur. Let cool. Arrange 1 cup miniature marshmallows over filling. Pour chocolate mixture over marshmallows. Refrigerate till serving.

Yield: 16-2 inch squares

Chocolate Chip Squares

ingredients:

½	cup	butter
1	cup	sugar
2		eggs
1½	cups	flour
¾	tsp	baking powder
2	Tbsp	cold water
¼	cup	Creme de Menthe Liqueur
1	cup	semi-sweet chocolate chips

method:

Preheat oven to 350° F.

Lightly grease a 9 inch square pan.

Cream butter and sugar. Beat in eggs one at a time. Sift together flour and baking powder. Mix together water and Creme de Menthe Liqueur. Add flour mixture alternately with water mixture, beat for about 2 minutes. Stir in chocolate chips. Spread into prepared pan. Bake for 20–25 minutes. Cut into squares while still warm.

Yield: 2 dozen squares

Cointreau Bundt Cake

ingredients:

2¼	cups	flour
½	tsp	salt
1½	tsp	baking powder
1	cup	butter
1½	cups	sugar
4		eggs
½	cup	Cointreau Liqueur
1	Tbsp	orange rind

method:

Preheat oven to 350° F.

Grease and flour a 8 cup bundt pan.

Sift together flour, baking powder and salt. Set aside.

Beat together butter, gradually add sugar and beat until light and fluffy. Add eggs, one at a time beating well after each. On low speed, add Cointreau Liqueur and flour mixture alternately. Beat in orange rind. Pour into prepared pan and bake for 50 minutes or until a toothpick inserted into the cake comes out clean. Remove from oven and let cool.

To serve, lightly dust with icing sugar.

Yield: 1 bundt cake

Mocha Almond Cheesecake

ingredients:

CRUST

1¼	cups	graham wafer crumbs
2	Tbsp	toasted almonds
¼	cup	cocoa
⅓	cup	butter

CHEESECAKE

2	8oz	(250g)pkgs cream cheese
¾	cup	sugar
¼	cup	cocoa
2		eggs
2	Tbsp	strong coffee
2	Tbsp	Swiss Chocolate Almond Liqueur
1	cup	sour cream
2	Tbsp	sugar
		toasted almond slivers
		chocolate curls

Mocha Almond Cheesecake

method:

Preheat oven to 350° F.

Combine graham wafer crumbs, toasted almonds and cocoa. Add the melted butter, mixing well. Press mixture into a 9 inch springform pan. Bake for 10 minutes. Let cool.

Beat together cream cheese and ¾ cup sugar until smooth. Beat in cocoa. Add eggs one at a time, beating well. Slowly beat in coffee. Pour over crust and bake for 35 minutes. Remove from oven.

Mix together Swiss Chocolate Almond Liqueur, sour cream and 2 Tbsp sugar. Spread over baked cheesecake. Bake for another 15 minutes. Remove from oven and let cool. Garnish with toasted almond slivers and chocolate curls.

Yield: 8–10 servings

Frozen Coolers

ingredients:

2	8oz	bottles or cans of Wine Cooler
1	8oz	can diet 7up
		soda water
		thinly sliced lemons or limes

method:

Mix together Wine Cooler and 7up in a freezable container. Place in freezer and freeze for 2–3 hours. When slushy, spoon into glasses and pour soda water over frozen mixture. Stir and serve. Garnish with lemon or lime slices.

Yield: 4 servings

METRIC CONVERSIONS

Volume:

¼ tsp	=	1ml
½ tsp	=	2ml
1 tsp	=	5ml
1 Tbsp	=	15ml
¼ cup	=	50ml
⅓ cup	=	75ml
½ cup	=	125ml
⅔ cup	=	150ml
¾ cup	=	175ml
1 cup	=	250ml

Weights:

¼ lb	=	125g
½ lb	=	250g
¾ lb	=	350g
1 lb	=	450g

Oven temperatures:

250° F	=	120° C
275° F	=	140° C
300° F	=	150° C
325° F	=	160° C
350° F	=	180° C
375° F	=	190° C
400° F	=	200° C
425° F	=	220° C
450° F	=	230° C

For information on obtaining additional copies of Liqueurs for Dessert, please send your name and address to:

Liqueurs for Dessert
P.O. Box 80956
Burnaby, B.C.
V5K 4K1